I Am
The Elements!

Written and Illustrated by

Aurora Lightbringer

D1711905

ISBN-13: 978-1499165890

ISBN-10:
1499165897

To Wren, my Nugget, of course!

And to Juliana and Will, Ellie and Dylan.

Love and light to our future leaders!

May magick be yours always!

I am the rain up in the clouds.

I am the drops falling down.

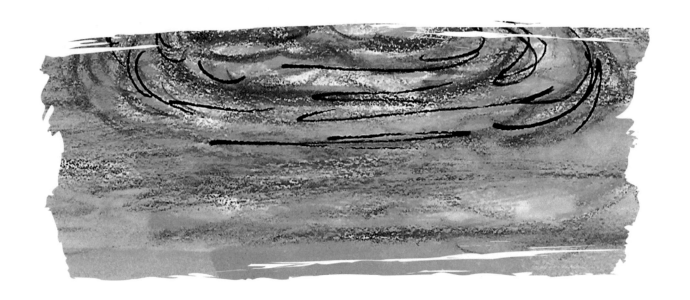

I am the ripples circling out.

I am intuition flowing 'round!

I am the Water,

spirit free!

As I will,

so mote it be!

I am the rocks, sand and stone.

I am the seed as it's sown.

I am the trees in the grove.

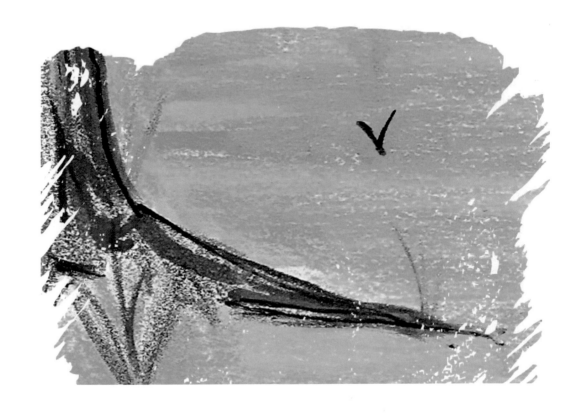

I am the grounding and the growth!

I am the Earth,

spirit free!

As I will,

so mote it be!

I am the air upon birds' wings.

I am a warm and fragrant breeze.

I am in sighs and whispering.

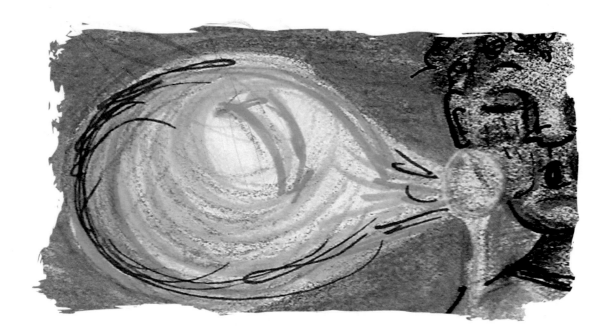

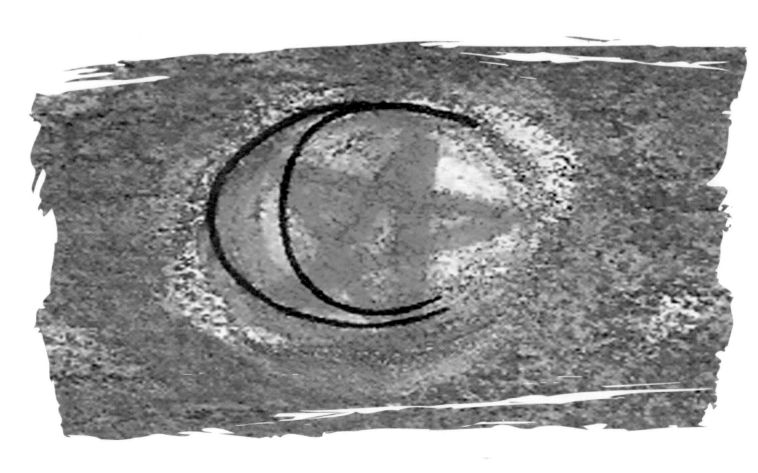

I am knowledge and learning!

I am the Air,

spirit free!

As I will,

so mote it be!

I am the spark that ignites.

I am glowing candlelight.

I am the sun shining bright.

I am power, strength and might!

I am the Fire,

spirit free!

As I will,

so mote it be!

We are the Elements, spirits free!

Merry meet and blessed be!

A note from the Author...

Why call the Elements?

Great question! There are many different traditions under the Pagan umbrella. Many of these traditions honor the Elements in some manner. Each of these traditions will explain the Elements a bit differently. Here's my simple way of explaining why we honor the Elements and call to them in our rituals…

The Elements remind us of two things: our connection to nature and our understanding that anything worth doing requires balanced energy. When we call the Elements in ritual we are acknowledging both things.

The following pages explain this a bit further and offer some suggestions for honoring the elements with children.

Air

Air connects us with the atmosphere that sustains life—the air that fills our lungs and the lungs of living things as well as the air that allows plants to breathe. There is even air in the water that fish breathe! Calling to Air connects us with flying creatures—birds, butterflies, and other bugs.

Air also represents knowledge and learning. Honoring Air reminds us that every endeavor requires some level of expertise and that part of transforming our dreams into reality is gaining the necessary knowledge to do so.

Honoring Air...

Take long, meditative breaths.

Blow bubbles!

Make a paper fan and feel the breeze it creates when you wave it around.

Fly a kite!

Observe birds and bugs.

Watch the clouds!

Eat fluffy foods like popcorn and cotton candy!

Read a book about something you are interested in.

Take a class about something that will help you achieve your goals!

Water

Water sustains all life— all living things need water to survive. Many of the Earth's most beautiful places were carved out by the power of Water over time. Calling to Water connects us with swimming creatures—fish, dolphins, otters, whales, crustaceans, and other sea and water life.

Water also represents emotions and intuition. Honoring Water reminds us that every endeavor requires some level of emotion to be committed to pursuing it and that part of transforming our dreams into reality is listening to our intuition along the way.

Honoring Water...

Drink a glass of cool ice water.

Paint with watercolors!

Water a plant.

Make a boat out of leaves and let it float down the stream or river.

Observe fish in their natural habitat or at an aquarium or zoo.

Play in the ocean!

Eat watery foods like watermelon and ice-pops!

Journal about your feelings.

Trust your intuition!

Fire

Fire connects us with the warmth that sustains life—the sun that allows plants and animals to live as well as the warmth our bodies create in living. Fire also helps us to create things—it turns sand into glass and clay into pottery; farmers sometimes burn fallow fields to create a fertile place to grow next year's crops. Calling to Fire connects us with crawling creatures that seek out warmth—salamanders, snakes, lizards and other reptiles.

Fire also represents passion and strength. Honoring Fire reminds us that every endeavor requires action and physical or mental strength and that part of transforming our dreams into reality is being strong enough to take the first step and persist along the way.

Honoring Fire...

Light a candle (with an adult's help).

Sit in the warmth of the Sun!

Make something out of clay—let it bake in a kiln or in the Sun.

Lift up rocks and logs and look for salamanders!

Roast marshmallows over the campfire (with an adult's help)!

Learn how to do a Sun Salutation yoga vinyasa!

Find something you are passionate about and practice it!

Earth

Earth connects us with the ground that supports and sustains life—the Earth beneath our feet, the sand at the beach, the soil that tree roots grow down into. Calling to Earth connects us with walking creatures—mostly mammals—as well as plants of all kinds.

Earth also represents grounding and growth. Honoring Earth reminds us that every endeavor we undertake will change us a bit and that part of transforming our dreams into reality is staying connected to things that ground and nurture us so we have the support we need to pursue our dreams.

Honoring Earth...

Touch the Earth with your hands.

Hold a crystal or rock in your hands!

Plant a tree.

Hug a tree!

Observe mammals—like squirrels—in their natural habitat or on animal preserves or zoos.

Eat local vegetables (better yet, eat them from your own garden)!

Find a quiet spot in your home or in nature that is your special place that you go to ground and center yourself.

About the Author

Aurora Lightbringer lives in Maryland where she enjoys painting and gardening and drumming by the campfire.

She is also a teacher and a mom and an advocate for Pagan kids in public schools. To read her recent article *Advocating for Pagan Children in the Public School System* please visit:

http://www.patheos.com/blogs/paganfamilies/2013/09/advocating-for-pagan-children-in-the-public-school-system/

Merry meet and merry part and merry meet again!

Made in the USA
Middletown, DE
15 June 2018